Don't Wait For the Perfect Moment.
Take the Moment and
Make It Perfect

– A THIRD COLLECTION OF POEMS BY
JOCELYN SHAFFER –

An environmentally friendly book printed and bound in England by
www.printondemand-worldwide.com

Mixed Sources
Product group from well-managed
forests, and other controlled sources
www.fsc.org Cert no. TT-COC-002641
© 1996 Forest Stewardship Council

PEFC Certified
This product is
from sustainably
managed forests
and controlled
sources
www.pefc.org
PEFC/16-33-415

This book is made entirely of chain-of-custody materials

www.fast-print.net/store.php

DON'T WAIT FOR THE PERFECT MOMENT.
TAKE THE MOMENT AND MAKE IT PERFECT
Copyright © Jocelyn Shaffer 2014

The right of Jocelyn Shaffer to be identified as the author of this work has
been asserted by her in accordance with the Copyright, Designs and
Patents Act 1988 and any subsequent amendments thereto.

A catalogue record for this book is available from the British Library

ISBN 978-178456-142-0

First published 2014 by
FASTPRINT PUBLISHING
Peterborough, England.

Contents

Poetry writing

One thing I love to do
Is poetry writing
Composing lots of rhymes
Can be so exciting

But sometimes though I try
I can't think up a rhyme
So patiently I try
And it comes to me in time

I'm now on my third book
It will appeal to some
I know I will be writing
For many years to come

If I don't like what I've written
I try not to get downhearted
I think of the ending
Before the poem's started!

It isn't always easy
To make the poem flow
So I leave it till the next day
Then have another go

I am so very pleased
When others get such pleasure
They buy my poetry book
And read it at their leisure

Jocelyn Shaffer

But one thing I must admit
And I am not pretending
It's my one and only poem
That I haven't got an ending!

Family history

There is a great hobby
That everyone can do
Researching family history
To find out who is who

It's a thrill to find out
You've got new relations
As you learn all about
The past generations

Searching public records
For evidence stored
Finding proof of relatives
May take you abroad

You may want to discover
If a family legend's true
Or if a famous person
Is related to you

Looking through papers
Whatever the weather
Is just like a jigsaw
Fitting pieces together

Others can join in
It makes it more fun
They help you with research
Until everything is done

Jocelyn Shaffer

You should use the internet
When you make your family tree
It's useful for updating
And is good for all to see

You may have some relatives
You didn't know existed
Found when you searched
In all the records listed

The more you research
The more relatives you discover
Until eventually you find
We're all related to each other!

Can't be me!

My birthday cards say sixty
I wonder who they're for
The postman must have got it wrong
When he came to my door

They surely can't be for me
The years have passed so quickly
It seems like only yesterday
When I had just turned fifty

I feel just like a teenager
Who goes clubbing all night long
It can't be me that's sixty
They must have got it wrong

I can run up and down the stairs
I don't use the escalator
I'm not in bed at midnight
As I stay up so much later

I like to watch the X factor
And hear the hopefuls sing
And it's always fun to watch
The judges arguing!

I've lots of friends on Facebook
And I text on my iphone
I join in lots of forums
Just to have a moan

Jocelyn Shaffer

I surely can't be sixty
I'm really rather fit
I like to go to coffee bars
Not stay home and knit!

I wear the latest fashions
And I look good in leather
So think of me as twenty one
I'm staying young forever!

Heyday

I was driving one morning
Down the main road
When suddenly I had to stop
A lorry lost its load

I wondered if I could help
And got out of my car
I rushed down the road
But didn't get very far

The lorry's load had spread
The road covered in hay
The traffic at a standstill
I'd be stuck there all day

The traffic got busier
And soon there was a queue
Not only were cars stuck
But buses and taxis too

The drivers got impatient
Didn't like being held up
Why weren't we moving?
And why are we stuck?

Then along came a policeman
And the hay he picked up
But couldn't do it all himself
So he called for some back-up

Jocelyn Shaffer

More policemen then arrived
So a long delay
One of them on a horse
Eating the hay!

The traffic was gridlocked
Couldn't move if they tried
Neither forward nor backward
Nor even to the side

Just then a gust of wind
Lifted up the hay
It floated over roof tops
Far, far away

At last the road was clear
The traffic again could flow
Everyone was pleased
So happy they could go

But on the other side of town
Drivers in a state
As hay was blocking their path
And they too would have to wait!

Intrusion

A chap at your front door
Wants to sell you crazy paving
If you go ahead today
10% you'd be saving!

Near the supermarket store
There's a man sat on the ground
He is begging for some money
So you give him a pound

In the home improvements
It's always the same
They always try to sell you
A new window frame?

You go to the market
You're approached by a guy
He has jewellery and watches
He wants you to buy

Then a chap comes up to you
When you are in the store
He wants to sell insurance
Before you reach the door

You walk down the street
A fellow blocks your way
He asks if you have the time
To do a quick survey

Jocelyn Shaffer

You go to the cinema
But as you reach the door
There's a beggar with a cap
Sitting cross-legged on the floor

You go to the theatre
All set to watch the show
They sell you a programme
And you feel you can't say no

You buy a raffle ticket
As many others have done
And although you didn't want it
You're delighted, as you've won!

Mountain climbing

Do you like mountain climbing?
Many people do
It is exhilarating
And very good for you

You have to go prepared
If you like to be outdoors
With brolly and a mac
Just in case it pours

You could be a hardcore climber
Pushing limits to the summit
Taking on a high mountain
So happy when you've done it

Some climbers are thrill seekers
Hoping to reach great heights
They make it up the mountain
And enjoy the sights

Sometimes there are avalanches
With rocks and falling stones
You have to be so careful
That you don't break any bones

And often the mountain route
Is strenuous and long
So you need to pace yourself
And be fit and strong

Jocelyn Shaffer

Some routes can be unsafe
So many climbers tripped
So make sure when you set off
That you are well equipped

You climb the highest mountain
And at the peak you stop
And in full view of everyone
You place your flag on top!

But the thrill of mountain climbing
Is not like any other
'Cos once you've reached the top of one
You're off to scale another!

Afternoon tea

An afternoon tea
Would be so very nice
My hubby suggested it
So I didn't think twice

So off we went
To the hotel in town
I dressed in my best
An afternoon gown

But when we arrived
Our table had been taken
We said that we had booked
And that he was mistaken

We showed a note we had
A receipt of our booking
He apologised and said
For a table he was looking

Eventually he found one
A small table that was free
He sat us down and went away
And we waited patiently

Half an hour passed
Then a waiter came with tea
But as he poured it out
It spilled all over me!

He rushed to wipe it up
But alas it was too late
I was soaking wet
And it did not feel great

He brought some sandwiches
But dropped them on the floor
He said that he would bring
Another plate with more

We waited quite a while
But a replacement never came
Although we kept reminding him
Time and time again

So we asked if we could have
A freshly made cream cake
He said that he would bring it
But yet another long wait

We saw that it had melted
As it was a hot day
It had sunk completely
Because of the delay

So we got up to go
And went towards the till
We had to pay the full amount
They would not reduce the bill

We handed them the cash
And waited whilst they checked it
They asked us for a tip
As the waiter would expect it

But there are times in life
When facts do need facing
So we gave a useful tip –
The waiter needs replacing!

I *am me*

I am as you see me
No frills or pretty bows
What you see is what you get
As everybody knows

I like to keep busy
And get everything done
And only then will I go out
And have lots of fun

I like meeting people
And am very sociable
I go to lots of places
And live life to the full

I like going shopping
And spending all my money!
I've a good sense of humour
And my jokes are quite funny

I am so very fond
Of poems that do rhyme
I would think up lots more of them
If I only had the time

I can be a bit impatient
I really don't mind stating
And I'm irritated
If I am kept waiting

I say how I feel
Sometimes without thinking
And launch into rhetoric
Without even blinking

So I am who I am
And I'll always be me
I know I'm not perfect
Although I strive to be

You take me as you find me
I will not change, it's true
But if you want a friend for life
I'm the one for you

Customer service

I'm hanging on the line
With music in my ears
Going slowly mad
As my patience disappears

I have been waiting ages
And breakfast is long gone
And now it's nearly two
And I am still holding on

I'm fifth in the queue
That's what I have been told
And they know that I'm waiting
And should continue to hold

The music is so annoying
What an awful noise
It's a big time waster
And is one of their ploys

My phone bill will be big
When I've finished this call
It is a prime time rate
And that's why they stall

And so I'm holding on
And now it's time for tea
I need to speak to someone
As quickly as can be

I've got a list of things
That I need to do
But I still have to hold
And wait till I get through

It really is annoying
And it's getting to me
Little did I know
How long the wait would be

At last it is my turn
I no longer feel dejected
They ask if they can help
Then I'm promptly disconnected!

Football crazy

I married a football player
But you can't call me a wag
I don't wear designer clothes
Nor an oversized bag!

I don't follow him around
Though he goes to every game
I don't worry if he's late
Nor do I watch him train

I stay in the background
And I never ever moan
'Cos if he is away from home
He finds time to telephone

I treat my man as equal
Which is how it should be
He can travel round the country
On his own without me

Although I don't like football
And I'd rather stay at home
I'm happy that he's playing
And don't mind that I'm alone

Although he's in the limelight
Every time he plays
I'm happy in the background
Away from public gaze

I know that he'll be faithful
He's just that kind of bloke
And if any girl comes on to him
He treats it as a joke

And when I said I'd marry him
No better match you'd get
He punched the air with joy
And shouted "Yeah, back of the net!"

Camping

Camping is a great hobby
And is very cheap too
It's stress free and relaxing
Something we should all do

You must take a map
In case of a wrong turn
So read up about camping
As there is a lot to learn

The weather may be changeable
So remember when you pack
To take some extra blankets
And, of course, a mac

There's time to enjoy nature
Like gazing up at stars
Or trailing through the woodlands
With no sign of bus or cars!

The more camping trips you make
The more that you will learn
Such as take a sunhat
So you don't get sunburn

And you should be considerate
No litter left around
Keep the site clean
No rubbish on the ground

And when the trip is over
And it's time to pack
You'll be planning to return
As soon as you get back!

House purchase

I wanted to move house
I felt that I should
Things can't stay the same
And a change would be good

So I went to the agents
And they showed me their list
I looked at all the properties
So hard to resist

They said there's a house
That was perfect for me
I was so excited
And couldn't wait to see

I arrived in good time
And went in to view
But the house was too large
And the garden was too

Then I saw another
It might have been alright
If I hadn't seen a crack
On the ceiling near the light

So the agent then arranged
Yet another house viewing
But it was just no use
As it needed too much doing

The next on the list
Had a very low ceiling
The pipes were leaking
And the wallpaper peeling

The kitchen was too big
In the next house I viewed
So I said my good byes
Not meaning to be rude

But now I am so happy
At long last I can rest
I'm staying where I am
As I like my own the best!

Age is just a number

Another birthday has arrived
And now I'm sixty four
Old age creeping ever closer
Something I ignore

I'm slowing down bit by bit
Can't do what I once could
And sometimes when I wake up
I really don't feel good

My eyesight isn't brilliant
So spectacles I wear
'Cos when I put my socks on
They're a different coloured pair!

I have many aches and pains
And wake up in the night
And toss and turn many times
Because I don't feel right

I slowly walk to catch a bus
To take me up to town
I really need to be cheered up
As I am feeling down

But an old man with a walking stick
Whose hair had gone white
Was shuffling behind me
In the morning light

But though I am sixty four
Life's good at every stage
As he called me a teenager
And wished he was my age!

Queen for a day

It would be so nice
To be Queen for a day
I'd have a great time
And rule my own way

I'd give all the guards
A day off to rest
And give them good food
And wine of the best

I'd give lots of money
To beggars and to strays
So that they wouldn't sleep
In alleys and doorways

I'd sit in my carriage
And wave to the crowd
They'd hold up their flags
And cheer very loud

But my life's not my own
Duties to perform
I have to be up early
Long before the dawn

And I cannot go shopping
Without being seen
Everything I do
Would be broadcast on screen

And I'd have to meet leaders
And travel quite a lot
And always reporters
Would be there on the spot

So all things considered
One thing I must say
I don't want to be Queen
For <u>more</u> than just a day!

Water, Water everywhere

I am just looking out
Through the window pane
The garden is wet
But there's no sign of rain

The leaves on the trees
Of which there are plenty
Have blown off the branches
And are dropping gently

The birds have all flown
To their nests in the trees
They don't like to be wet
Although they like the breeze

The hedgerows and grass
Are now very wet
It makes them grow tall
The more water they get

The flowers are all blooming
When they're wet they grow
And their petals will open
The higher that they go

But all of the insects
Have now gone into hiding
They will soon re-appear
When the water's subsiding

I see that the day
Is now looking bright
And it's getting warmer
As the sun comes out

The window is now dry
There's no sign of rain
But I know that tomorrow
It will be wet again

Of this there is no doubt
As it will be that way
Because my water sprinkler
Is turned on every day!

Interruptions

There was a good thriller
On the TV one day
Every minute was exciting
Couldn't tear myself away

And then the phone rang
It was my Auntie Ray
She wanted to chat
And had a lot to say

So after the call
I went back to watch TV
I'd missed quite a bit
But the rest I would see

Then the doorbell rang
I was tempted to ignore it
But the caller persisted
So there was nothing for it

I opened the door
A salesman said 'hello'
Will I purchase new windows?
And he just wouldn't go

I said I didn't want
And then shut the door
And went back to the thriller
And settled down for more

But the phone rang again
He said his name was Jim
It was a cold caller
I could not get rid of him

And whilst I'd been away
I'd missed how it finished
The excitement that I'd felt
Very soon diminished

So if anyone out there
Would like to help a friend
Please let me know
Just how did it end?

A quiet chat

I went out to a café
It was in the West End
Just for a quiet chat
And coffee with my friend

All was going well
Until a party came in
They sat down nearby
And made such a din

Shrieking and laughing
All the girls and boys
Had to shout to be heard
They were making such a noise

It was someone's birthday
They were singing along
And all the other diners
Sang the birthday song

Then someone got drunk
He had been drinking beer
And the shouting and the yelling
Went up a another gear

And then there was a lull
Perhaps some peace at last
But piped music started playing
Which was put on at full blast

It was all just too much
We got up and went out
This wasn't what I wanted
Didn't think I'd have to shout

What started as a quiet chat
Has brought me close to tears
My voice is really hoarse
And I've ringing in my ears!

Next time I want a quiet chat
Without an awful din
I'll invite my friend to my house
And we will just stay in!

Kitchen Bridge

I like to play bridge
Whenever I am free
Much more interesting
Than watching TV

We sit around the table
All four of us in place
We all follow suit
As defender leads an ace

But as I'm concentrating
Someone wants a break
So we agree to continue
After tea and cake

So we start chatting
And time marches on
And then before we know it
The evening has gone

We go back to our cards
But I've lost my concentration
I've forgotten who played what
With the social conversation

So now I am resigned
To playing just a little
As so much time is taken
By the break in the middle

So we leave with no result
And it's always the same
Will we ever get to finish
Even one bridge game!

But now I have the answer
The next time we meet
After setting up the table
And taking a seat

We put the kettle on
And then raid the fridge
Yes, the only thing to do
Is forget about the bridge!

The house fly

There was a little house fly
It flew in through the door
It landed on the window sill
Then flew down to the floor

It crawled along the carpet
And up the wooden chair
Then flew around the room
Looking for fresh air

I took a piece of paper
To help it on its way
To make sure that this was
A very short stay

But as it neared the paper
It turned and crawled away
I tried in vain to coax it
But it just wouldn't stay

Round and round the room
It circled to and fro
It did not seem to know
Which way that it should go

I thought that if I drew the blinds
To take away the light
It would fly towards the door
Outside where it was bright

But sadly this did not work
It still flew all about
So I opened the window wide
To try to coax it out

Eventually it found the way
It flew out really fast
I was so very pleased
That it was free at last

My efforts had been worthwhile
And the fly now was free
It was no longer trapped indoors
But where it's meant to be

But as I closed the window
As the fly had departed
Another one flew in
So now I'm back where I started!

Washing day

It really is a guessing game
When you hang your washing out
'Cos when you've pegged the last one
Oh no, there's rain about!

But if the washing's not outside
Just in case it pours
No doubt the sun will come out
Whilst your washing's wet indoors!

I'm in and out a hundred times
At every sign of rain
I bring the washing back indoors
Then hang them out again!

Some clothes may be a little damp
So I air them inside
The rest can be put away
As they are fully dried

I hang them on the washing line
Before I get the train
But I'm loathe to leave them outdoors
Just in case of rain

I could take them to the launderette
It isn't far away
But it's time consuming
As I'm washing every day

But now my problem has been solved
And we should all acquire
No more wet washing to hang out
I've got a tumble dryer!

Jocelyn Shaffer

Summer barbeque

It's nice to have a barbeque
In the summer time
Chatting with all our friends
In the warm sunshine

But which day to make it
Is quite a guessing game
Even if it's nice one day
Would the next be the same?

If the weather forecast's good
Can we go by what they say?
They've been known to get it wrong
And it's rained all day

When my friends have barbeques
The weather has been fine
They always seem to get it right
But I don't, when I have mine!

We plan a summer barbeque
On a sunny night
But then the rain starts to fall
In the fading light

And then when it's pouring down
We call off the barbeque
And too late to re-arrange
When the sky turns blue

So there's only one thing for it
Even if it pours
We'll still have a barbeque
But it'll have to be indoors!

The cost of bread!

One day I had run out of bread
So I went to buy some more
I wrote out a shopping list
And drove to the superstore

And so I went up all the aisles
To take all that I need
My basket completely full
A large family to feed

When I was done, I went to pay
For my grocery shopping
And then I loaded up my car
There was no time for stopping

So I drove home, very pleased
The family will be fed
But when I arrived I realised
I'd forgotten to buy the bread!

So off I went once again
Just to my local shop
It shouldn't take me very long
As it's a moment's stop

I went in and took my bread
And then I went to pay
But I had left my purse at home
It just was not my day

I had to leave the bread behind
Though I needed it for tea
And a parking ticket on my car
What a day for me

With thoughts of my forgetfulness
Running through my head
Time wasted and a parking fine
And I hadn't any bread

And then I had the answer
As I set off for home
I'll never need to buy more bread
As I'm going to make my own!

Too many warnings

Why is it that things we like
Are always bad for us
We are told that we should walk
When we'd rather catch a bus

We go abroad to hot countries
As we don't like the rain
But we are told to cover up
So wonder why we came

They say that too much chocolate
Is bad for us to eat
We'll only end up getting fat
And should avoid that treat

Mobile phones and computers
Are always in the news
They give off radiation
And are quite a risk to use

And there are warnings
About eating too much meat
Likewise pasta and white rice
In fact anything with wheat

And watching television
Isn't good because we're sat
We become couch potatoes
And end up very fat

And even too much exercise
Is something that is frowned on
Too much, wears out our joints
Too little, puts the pounds on

One day they say something's good
Next day they say it's bad
We just don't know what to believe
It might be a passing fad

But the happiest of people
In health they are the strongest
They ignore all advice
And they always live the longest!

First thing you do

What is the first thing that you do
The moment you wake up
Do you brew yourself some tea
Then have a second cup?

Perhaps you do some exercise
And stretch out every limb
Or do you just rush out of bed
And head off to the gym?

Perhaps you go down the stairs
And turn on your PC
Or switch on your mobile phone
Or sit down and watch TV?

Do you wake your partner
To remind him of his meeting
And quickly make his breakfast
If he has time for eating?

Perhaps it takes you ages
To get out of your warm bed
Or you may get up too quickly
Your dog needs to be fed

Do you open wide the curtains
And then your window pane
Even though the chances are
That there will be some rain

Do you rush to the bathroom
To shower and then get dressed
As you like to start the day
Making sure you look your best

Do you want to know what I do?
Well I don't exercise or snack
As all I do when I wake up
Is turn over and go back!

Can't see!

I booked for the theatre
I couldn't wait to go
It had very good reviews
And would be a great show

I arrived in good time
And I'd only just sat
When a lady sat in front
Wearing a big hat

I asked if she'd remove it
As it blocked my view
She seemed quite offended
And said she wouldn't do

So I got up to move
And looked all around
And hoped that a spare seat
Quickly could be found

But just as I stood up
The man behind me in a rage
Said 'would you please sit down
As I can't see the stage'

So I sat back down again
And leant to my right
I could see half the stage
But it wasn't my night

As the lady next to me
Told me to sit up straight
She didn't like me leaning
Or she'd raise a complaint

So I bent to my left
It was the only way
But the chap on my left
Said I couldn't stay

I then resigned myself
To having no view at all
There was nothing I could do
As I wasn't very tall

So I'll have to be up early
Next time I want a treat
I'll be first in the queue
To buy a front row seat!

The news

I wake up in the morning
Feeling quite refreshed
I have a wash and clean my teeth
And then quickly I get dressed

I go downstairs for breakfast
Then the newspaper I read
The news is so depressing
And something I don't need

The postman has delivered
So I rush to the door
But there are loads of bills
And I'm depressed once more

I turn on the TV
For something that's light hearted
But headlines are there too
That more wars have started

I pick up my iphone
A message there recorded
A gift has been cancelled
That earlier I'd ordered.

I go to my computer
Events have filtered through
Another war has started
I guess that's nothing new

I turn on the radio
For a soothing melody
But war headlines interrupt
Why can't I be news-free

So I've decided that tomorrow
I'll do nothing all of the day
No papers, no phone or PC
As no news is good news they say!

Dilemma

I was asked to write an article
For a popular magazine
About people that I knew
Or places that I'd seen

I was so excited
Couldn't hide my delight
So I sat down with pad and pen
And thought of what to write

I could write about politics
And items in the news
But that's a tricky subject
As others have their views

I could write about the fellow
Who worked in radio
Or about the actor
In a popular TV show

I could write about the time I had
When I went on a cruise
And all the people that I met
And the amazing views

I could write about the strange tale
That a friend recently related
It was funny at the time
But perhaps now outdated

Or when I was going away
And my dog was out all night
He was nowhere to be found
So I missed my next day flight

I could write about my hobbies
Many started long ago
Very interesting to me
But would others find them so

So I never wrote an article
Though I thought from day to night
Too many topics to choose from
Couldn't decide what to write!

A fair catch

There's something about a fair
That is so appealing
I am a child at heart
And it gives me a good feeling

I like to go on all the rides
The dodgems are the best
I drive and bump and have such fun
I've passed my driving test!

And then I spot the roundabout
With horses going round
Up they go and down again
They never make a sound

And then the big dipper
It really is a thrill
All the world is going round
Nothing keeping still!

I really want a cuddly toy
Not an easy task
I steer the crane to pick it up
But falls from my grasp

And then I try another stall
And close my eyes and wish
I throw a dart at the board
And win a prize goldfish!

It's put into a tiny bag
Not much room to swim
But I'm pleased I have it
It was really nice to win

Going home, the water splashed
So I tried to keep it still
My fish just swam around
Though some of it did spill

I put it in a large bowl
Changed the water every day
I gave it food and watched it eat
But alas it passed away

I loved my little goldfish
It was really like no other
So I'm going to the fair again
So I can win another!

Getting away to the sunshine!

I set off for a one week break
The sun was shining brightly
But when I arrived it had gone dull
And rain was falling lightly

The second day the sun was out
For the beach I was all set
But on the way the rain came down
And I got very wet

The third day looked like being nice
At last there was no rain
But very soon the sky went dull
And rain came down again

The fourth day of my holiday
Started off so bright
But rain came down just as the beach
Was almost in my sight

The fifth day of my holiday
Began very warm
So I was not prepared at all
For the sudden heavy storm

The sixth day of my holiday
Was a real wash out
The storm clouds kept gathering
And rain was all about

And so the final day arrived
I left the beach behind
My one week's holiday over
The weather had been unkind

How unlucky I had been
There'd been rain every day
It had spoiled my holiday
In every single way

But as I reached my own front door
I felt the sun's warm rays
It shone brightly in the sky
And stayed out for seven days!

In perspective

The house is in a state
And the walls needed painting
The curtains are all frayed
And carpets need replacing

The floorboards are creaking
And the back door is stuck
The fitted oven has broken down
So no way can I cook

The tiles are all cracked
On the bathroom wall
And the light switch has broken
Near the front door in the hall

The grout is discoloured
In the shower cubicle
And there's a large crack
In the bathroom pedestal

But tomorrow no doubt will be
A better day I'm sure
And I won't be complaining
Nor will I ask for more

I won't care about the house
Nor the state it's in
Nor whether it needs painting
Nor emptying the bin

Nor the broken tiles
Or the faulty light
It really doesn't matter
If nothing is put right

I've come to a decision
Something that won't fail
I am looking for a new house
As this one's up for sale!

Football mad

My boyfriend's mad on football
Although we don't agree
But I know he'll never change
And that's how it's meant to be

And when his team has won,
There's a smile on his face
But if he is looking sad
I know that's not the case

If we've booked an evening meal
And then his team is beaten
He just won't leave the house
Even though we haven't eaten

And sometimes when we've planned
To go out to the pictures
He has to check it doesn't clash
With the weekend's fixtures

Even if a close friend
Has booked her wedding day
There's no way he will go
If his team are going to play

Our social life depends
On every single match
As he won't make any plans
If they're on a bad patch

Football's all he lives for
He'll never miss a game
And he never gets bored
As no two are the same

We have to plan our holidays
For that very reason
He will only go away
At the end of the season

I'd love him to propose to me
And wouldn't ask for more
So this afternoon I beg of you
Mr Rooney, please score!

Nothing could be better

Our grandsons live out of town
A three hours' drive away
So we were so excited
When they came to stay

They were so delightful
Such lovely little boys
They happily settled down
And played with all their toys

The house was upside down
Toys scattered all around
And when they were both in bed
We tried not to make a sound

We took them to the seaside
They had a great time
Though at times it was overcast
The weather did stay fine

Aunt and uncles came around
Their two nephews to see
They had lots of fun with them
And they stayed for tea

Meal times were chaotic
With so many to cater for
But they all lent a hand
So we couldn't have asked for more

It was hard when it was time to go
And we had to say goodbye
It was always at times like these
That we wished they lived nearby

But although we were really sad
What stopped us feeling blue
Was when they said before they left
Grandma, Grandpa we love you)))

Most memorable

Which day was most memorable?
Can you remember?
Was it your birthday
Or the fifth of November

Perhaps it was the day
You passed your driving test
Though at the time you thought
You hadn't done your best

Or it may have been the day
That your wedding vows were said
You drank too much wine
Which went straight to your head!

Or it could have been the day
That your team won the cup
You rejoiced all through the day
But all night you were up

It might have been when you went
On holiday to Rome
You had such a great time
You didn't want to come home

Or was it playing football
On a day that was wet
When you headed the ball
Into the corner of the net

Or when you had played golf
And all day the sun had shone
You were so delighted
When you got a hole in one

Or it might have been the day
You gained your degree
That really was a day
That you thought you'd never see

So make the most of life
And every moment treasure
And then EVERY day will be
Your greatest day ever!

Forgetfulness

I can be so forgetful
When I put things away
I put them in a cupboard
But forget where next day

Then later when I want them
They're nowhere to be found
I look in all the drawers
And then search all around

When I put things away
I use different places
But then when I want them
I have lost all traces

So many things go missing
It really puzzles me
And when they do turn up
They're not where they're meant to be

It really is a problem
I wonder what to do
I've mislaid all my old things
And will have to buy more new

But now I have the answer
And I have no more to fear
I'm jotting down each item
So they will not disappear

So I wrote down all the items
So nothing would be missed
But things have gone from bad to worst
As I've gone and lost my list!

Weight watching

My weight has been creeping up
A stone I have to lose
So I need a diet plan
Which one should I choose

Perhaps a vegan diet
Would help me lose the weight
No dairy, honey, eggs
But there'd be nothing on my plate!

My friend said try the Atkins diet
You'll lose weight, you'll see
It's based on very low carbs
But I don't think it's for me

The cabbage soup diet's popular
And easy to prepare
But it is really not for me
As cabbage, I can't bear!

The grapefruit diet's a good one
My friend said, you will see
But more than one grapefruit
Will soon go straight through me!

What about a Gluten free
Based on barley, rye and wheat
But although it is quite healthy
It's not what I want to eat

If I try a crash diet
My weight will soon diminish
But it will all come back again
The moment that I finish

But now I have decided
Which diet it will be
With a cream cake in each hand
A balanced diet's for me!

Reunion

Whilst reading the newspaper
An advert I did see
For a school reunion
At a hall not far from me

It was very tempting
I wondered should I go
But would they know who I was
From my class so long ago

I thought about it carefully
It would be nice to see
Many of my old friends
From my class of Sixty three

So I put on my best clothes
Perhaps overdressed a touch
But hoped that when they saw me
I hadn't changed too much

Seeing them, after so long
It would be strange, I know
And hearing how life's treated them
From those days long ago

Lots of catching up to do
And stories to be told
Would we remember what we did
As we're all getting old

Then off I went to meet them all
I took my camera too
And as I got near to the hall
My excitement grew and grew

But not a soul I recognised
Amongst everyone I saw
How could I have got it oh so wrong
My class was Sixty four!

Infections

There are many ailments
That anyone can get
Even just a common cold
If you get too wet

Many are infectious
Such as chicken pox
Or even German measles
You would know by the spots

And coughs and colds also
Are easily passed on
Especially if the carrier
Has sneezed near you and then gone

And there are bugs that lurk
They can make you feel funny
You should be careful what you eat
As they cause an upset tummy

And there are many viruses
That quite often lay you low
You need antibiotics
But takes ages to go

An infection can incubate
So you don't know that you've got it
Then a few days later
You wake up, very spotted

But there is something infectious
That I'm happy if I get
Smiling is infectious
And the best infection yet!

A bagful of problems

I carry lots in my bag
Whenever I go out
As there are many items
That I couldn't be without

I always take my credit cards
If I go to a store
Even though I carry cash
I might just need some more

And of course my house keys
Are safely put away
And some bottled water
If it's a warm day

And I take my purse
Can't leave that behind
And chequebook and pen
So they can be signed

And I take my make-up
On a journey far away
As I might need to freshen up
Later on that day

And as my hands feel the cold
Gloves are put in too
Along with lots of tissues
In case I catch the flu!

And I take my sun glasses
To keep out harmful rays
As shades are very useful
On our summer days

My hair brush if it's windy
Is something that I take
And a pack of pain killers
In case of a headache

I also take some plasters
To use if I stumble
And a snack in my bag
For a tummy rumble

My fold-up brolly I must take
And in the bag it goes
I always take it with me
In case it rains or snows

My diary has to be to hand
So many things to note
Just in case I might forget
Something that I wrote!

But sadly all my things won't fit
What shall I leave behind
It really is a problem
I can't make up my mind

Jocelyn Shaffer

So please tell me what to do
As nothing more will fit
My bag is bursting at the seams
Stretched to the limit

But now I have it sorted
Such an easy thing to do
I've bought a larger bag
It fits my phone and charger too!

But a big bag can cause problems
As sadly I have found
As my back is now aching
From carrying it around!

An upgrade

I wanted to upgrade my phone
It was a few years old
And better ones were now about
And many had been sold

I went on to the internet
To log into my account
But I couldn't access it
It seemed I'd been locked out

I requested a new password
One that I had not used
They gave a link to click on
But each time it was refused

I tried to find a number
To phone them or to text
But there were none to be found
To telephone them direct

I tried to send an e-mail
But nothing there at all
Impossible to get in touch
So couldn't write or call

At last I found a number
A premium one at that
I intended to be brief
With the minimum of chat

I was kept holding on for ages
How long would it be?
Eventually they answered
But they could not help me

They said that they would send
Another password code
So I tried to access it
But it just wouldn't load

By then, I'd had enough
I was so frustrated
I was getting nowhere
And so exasperated

They said they'd let me know
Why my account was locked
And why I couldn't access it
Because it had been blocked

They didn't seem to know
Though they said I hadn't used it
So it had been removed
In case others abused it!

I told them it was current
I've a contract which I pay
I'm locked out of my account
And need it use it right away

But they still couldn't help
What more could I do
So I can't change my phone
For one that is brand new

So I'm keeping my phone
Even though it is dated
I tell myself that mine is fine
New ones are overrated!

Getting older

I know I'm getting older
My teeth are not so white
I'm slow at getting out of bed
And I'm losing height

I know I'm getting older
I'm sleeping all the time
My memory isn't what it was
I can't think up a rhyme!

I know I'm getting older
I can't walk very far
And when I want to see a friend
I drive there in my car

I know I'm getting older
I sleep later in the day
Everything takes longer
And my hair is turning grey

I know I'm getting older
Everything's a chore
Lines are showing on my face
And my feet are sore

I know I'm getting older
And I know that I'm not fit
It's hard to walk up the stairs
As I would rather sit

I know I'm getting older
I find it hard to hear
And now I cannot read a book
Unless I hold it near

I know I'm getting older
And aches and pains are plenty
But though I look my sixty years
Inside I'm only twenty!

Telephone interruptions

It was a busy day
My work would be double
I had to get it done
Or I would be in trouble

I began my first task
But then I heard the phone
No time to answer
So ignored the ringtone

But it wouldn't stop
So I had to pick it up
It was a cold caller
So I knew I was stuck

At last he cleared the line
I was glad that he had gone
But then it rang again
And I couldn't carry on

This time is was a friend
Who just wanted to chat
I told her I was busy
But she ignored that

She talked and talked for ages
And I really fell behind
So I had to say goodbye
And hoped she didn't mind

Then I got back to my work
I'd hardly done a thing
But just as I got down to it
The telephone did ring

I didn't want to answer it
As I had so much to do
It rang and rang incessantly
So I had to find out who

This time it was a PC guy
Said a virus in my computer
He just wouldn't get off the line
Said he's a trouble shooter

I told him my PC's fine
And to leave me alone
I said I would report him
If he didn't get off the phone

At last I got rid of him
But it was getting late
Lots of work to be done
And I was getting in a state

Then my boss telephoned
I told him I'd been delayed
He said I had to do the work
Or I would not get paid

Jocelyn Shaffer

I didn't like his attitude
Told him I didn't care
I didn't want to work for him
And said I'd look elsewhere

And now, it's two weeks later
I've a job with better pay
I'm a telephone receptionist
And making calls all day!

Golden oldies

I couldn't find my spectacles
I'd been looking high and low
I'd looked everywhere
Had nowhere else to go

Had they dropped on the floor
Or been put behind a book?
Were they in a bottom drawer?
Where else could I look

Had I left them on the bus
When I went in the shop?
And I put them on to see
The cost of my new top

Did they fall out of my bag
When I took them off?
To have a drink of water
As I had a cough

Were they on the table
When I went to the door
Or were they in the kitchen
And had fallen to the floor

And so I was still looking
When my sister came in
I said 'I'd lost my glasses'
And she began to grin

Jocelyn Shaffer

You're wearing them, she said
It's easy to see
And then I remembered
How forgetful I could be

So it now looks like the time
To join the enrolments
Of the elite group of citizens
Who have had senior moments!

Tennis

My boyfriend's love is tennis
Can't get enough of it
I have to help him practice
Though I'd really rather sit

He follows all the matches
And plays when he can
And when it comes to Wimbledon
He is the biggest fan

If my partner wins a game
I cheer with all the rest
I'm really happy for him
As I know that he's the best

He sometimes dreams of tennis
In his sleep he hits an ace
I never wake him up
As he's in a nice place

His follows the top players
As he aspires to be the same
He has lots of practice
To improve his game

I sometimes go to watch him
Though I do get rather bored
But it's nice to see his fans
Cheering and applaud

Jocelyn Shaffer

Other girls come on to him
They think that he is free
But he has no interest in them
Which soon they plainly see

And though my boyfriend knows
I'm no tennis devotee
Though it's love all in tennis
It's love only me!

A right to sleep

On Monday I was kept awake
A police helicopter overhead
It started flying to and fro
Just as I went to bed
It circled round for two hours
With it's bright and shining light
No doubt searching for someone
Who had got into a fight

On Tuesday I was kept awake
An alarm began to wail
It really was annoying
As that house was up for sale
And it rang for ages
I had hoped the noise would cease
So that I could settle down
And finally get some peace

On Wednesday I was kept awake
A dog barking down the lane
The owners had left it out
And it had begun to rain
It barked and barked for ages
And made such a din
That our other neighbours' quiet dog
Decided to join in!

Jocelyn Shaffer

On Thursday I was kept awake
A party on till 4
With pop music on full volume
It should be against the law
Lots of voices filled the air
Shrieking with delight
And there were car doors slamming
So no sleep for me that night

When Friday came at last some peace
But this just can't be right
Loud booms and bangs filled the air
Oh no, it's Bonfire night!

I am what I am

I'm happy in my own skin
What you see is what you get
Others have enhancements
Which in time they may regret

I don't want my breasts enlarged
I'm happy with my size
And it doesn't bother me
If I've bags under my eyes

Some pay to have their teeth done
And even take a loan
Though mine are not perfect
They are still all my own

I don't wear six inch heels
They're more like stilts than shoes
And you can keep your body art
As I'm not into tattoos

I don't want body piercings
Especially down below!
And my eyebrows don't need threading
I use my thread to sew!

I'm not a slave to fashion
I like my own taste
Designer bags cost the earth
They're really such a waste

Jocelyn Shaffer

I do not want botox
Pricked lips that cannot grin
And I don't want a face lift
If I get a double chin!

But though I'm happy as I am
One thing that I must hide
You won't see me in public
Until my roots are dyed!

On strike

I'm going on strike
As I'm tired of doing dishes
I'm tired of catering
To everybody's wishes

I'm going on strike
It has to be this way
I've done enough cleaning
Every single day

I'm going on strike
As it's getting tough
I'm having a break
'Cos enough is enough

I'm going on strike
I may have been admired
But now I'm getting older
And feeling very tired

I'm going on strike
I need to have a rest
I hope you don't mind
As it is for the best

I'm going on strike
As I'm busy night and day
And you know the old saying
All work and no play

Jocelyn Shaffer

I'm going on strike
It's been long overdue
I need to have a break
Where there's nothing to do

I'm going on strike
It may fill you with sorrow
But please don't shed a tear
'Cos I'll be back tomorrow!

Pill problem

I'd had a bad migraine
Of a long duration
So I went to the pharmacist
For some medication

The pharmacist suggested
Which pills I should take
He said they were good
And would cure my headache

'You should take three a day'
The pharmacist had said
They will definitely relieve
Your poor aching head

So I picked up the pills
And decided to buy them
And then rushed home
And got ready to try them

I must not do any driving
Said a label inside
Though I had no intention
Of going for a ride

It said there may be side effects
When on these pills
But I'm sure no one wants
Any unpleasant ills

Jocelyn Shaffer

The side effects were listed
There were so many points
Dizziness and rashes
And aching joints

I was now a bit worried
Because there were so many
If the pills could cause them
Perhaps I shouldn't take any

And so I rang my sister
And told her what I bought
I read out the instructions
To see what she thought

She said before I took them
I should ring the pharmacist
And read out the side effects
On that long list

So I rang him up
He said I should take them
Because if they weren't safe
They just wouldn't make them

And so I took one out
In view of what he said
But should I take it after food
Or just before bed?

And should I take it with water?
Or with a cup of tea?
As I hadn't been told
When time it should be

It said 'take three a day'
So I must get it right
Should I set my alarm
For a pill in the night?

Or should I take all three
During the day?
It would be so much easier
To do it that way

But then another problem
And one I can't control
The pill was much too big
To be swallowed whole

So it needed crunching up
So that I can take it
Had to hope it wasn't hard
For me to break it

So I broke it in two pieces
But it needed more
Then the chopped up pill
Fell to bits on the floor

Jocelyn Shaffer

I unwrapped another pill
But decided not to break it
My migraine had gone now
So there was no need to take it!

A wanted visitor

My cat is called Alfie
I found him as a stray
He was sitting outside
On my doorstep one day

I tried to find his owner
But no one replied
So from that day on
He's been by my side

He made a mess all over
And sat on the settee
He jumped up on the table
And scratched my new TV

His fur was on my clothing
And hairs upon the chairs
All day I had to clean up
Both up and down the stairs

He was sick when I fed him
So to the vet I went
He needed medication
And lots of money spent

He slept in my bedroom
Didn't like to sleep alone
He was always beside me
When I was on the phone

He liked to be tickled
Just under his chin
And he put on some weight
Though he was never thin

But though he caused problems
Almost every day
I really wouldn't want him
Any other way!

But then his owner came
And said he had tried
To find his little cat
And spotted him outside

I said that I'd advertised
Far and wide
But no one came forward
So he'd stayed by my side

He thanked me repeatedly
But 'twas hard to part
With my sweet little Alfie
Who'd captured my heart

But I had no choice
And had to say goodbye
It was hard to see him go
And I tried not to cry

And so I gave him back
With a heavy heart
It was going to be tough
For us to be apart

That night I was sad
And missed him so much
I hoped that his owner
Would still keep in touch

But next day to my surprise
On the outside mat
I found sitting there
Another stray cat

But I don't want marks
Or scratches on my chair
Nor lots of hair
On everything I wear

Nor my house a mess
And my bed not my own
If this cat was like Alfie
And wouldn't sleep alone

I couldn't do it again
Then have a broken heart
If the owner came back
It would tear me apart

But he looked so cute
As I went to close the door
'Alright, come in,' I said
What are you waiting for!!

A writing lull

My poems give such pleasure
I write them at my leisure
And even if I haven't time
I'll still jot down a funny rhyme

And if a verse comes in my head
Even if it's time for bed
Out comes my pen and I will write
Even if it's in the night

And sometimes if I am out shopping
And I do not feel like stopping
If I think of one, I'll write it down
Even in the heart of town

But though I've written oh so many
Today I just can't think of any
I've wracked my brains a hundred times
To come up with some funny lines

I've written lots in the past
And some I've written very fast
But now nothing comes to mind
I've thought and thought but nothing's rhymed

I can't think what to write about
All ideas have now run out
I wish that I could feel inspired
But all I am is very tired

Jocelyn Shaffer

I will write more, but don't know when
Tomorrow I shall try again!
It's not often that I am stuck
So look out for my fourth book!